A Note From Rick Renner

I am on a personal quest to see a "revival of the Bible" so people can establish their lives on a firm foundation that will stand strong and endure the test as end-time storm winds begin to intensify.

In order to experience a revival of the Bible in your personal life, it is important to take time each day to read, receive, and apply its truths to your life. James tells us that if we will continue in the perfect law of liberty — refusing to be forgetful hearers, but determined to be doers — we will be blessed in our ways. As you watch or listen to the programs in this series and work through this corresponding study guide, I trust you will search the Scriptures and allow the Holy Spirit to help you hear something new from God's Word that applies specifically to your life. I encourage you to be a doer of the Word He reveals to you. Whatever the cost, I assure you — it will be worth it.

> Thy words were found, and I did eat them;
> and thy word was unto me the joy and rejoicing of mine heart:
> for I am called by thy name, O Lord God of hosts.
> — Jeremiah 15:16

Your brother and friend in Jesus Christ,

Rick Renner

What the New Testament Tells Us About Demons

Copyright © 2019 by Rick Renner
1814 W. Tacoma St.
Broken Arrow, OK 74012-1406

Published by Rick Renner Ministries
www.renner.org

ISBN 13: 978-1-6803-1613-1

ISBN 13 eBook: 978-1-6803-1651-3

How To Use This Study Guide

This five-lesson study guide corresponds to *"What the New Testament Says About Demons" With Rick Renner* (**Renner TV**). Each lesson in this study guide covers a topic that is addressed during the program series, with questions and references supplied to draw you deeper into your own private study of the Scriptures on this subject.

To derive the most benefit from this study guide, consider the following:

First, watch or listen to the program prior to working through the corresponding lesson in this guide. (Programs can also be viewed at **renner.org** by clicking on the Media/Archives links or on our Renner Ministries YouTube channel.)

Second, take the time to look up the scriptures included in each lesson. Prayerfully consider their application to your own life.

Third, use a journal or notebook to make note of your answers to each lesson's Study Questions and Practical Application challenges.

Fourth, invest specific time in prayer and in the Word of God to consult with the Holy Spirit. Write down the scriptures or insights He reveals to you.

Finally, take action! Whatever the Lord tells you to do according to His Word, do it.

For added insights on this subject, it is recommended that you obtain Rick Renner's book *Dressed To Kill*. You may also select from Rick's other available resources by placing your order at **renner.org** or by calling 1-800-742-5593.

TOPIC

The Demoniac of Gadara

SCRIPTURES

1. **Luke 10:17-19** — And the seventy returned again with joy, saying, Lord, even the devils are subject unto us through thy name. And he said unto them, I beheld Satan as lightning fall from heaven. Behold, I give unto you power to tread on serpents and scorpions, and over all the power of the enemy....

2. **Isaiah 14:12** — How art thou fallen from heaven, O Lucifer, son of the morning! how art thou cut down to the ground, which didst weaken the nations!

3. **Ezekiel 28:16** — By the multitude of thy merchandise they have filled the midst of thee with violence, and thou hast sinned: therefore I will cast thee as profane out of the mountain of God: and I will destroy thee, O covering cherub, from the midst of the stones of fire.

4. **1 John 4:4** — Ye are of God, little children, and have overcome them: because greater is he that is in you, than he that is in the world.

5. **Mark 5:1-5** — And they came over unto the other side of the sea, into the country of the Gadarenes. And when he was come out of the ship, immediately there met him out of the tombs a man with an unclean spirit. Who had his dwelling among the tombs; and no man could bind him, no, not with chains. Because that he had been often bound with fetters and chains, and the chains had been plucked asunder by him, and the fetters broken in pieces: neither could any man tame him. And always, night and day, he was in the mountains, and in the tombs, crying, and cutting himself with stones.

GREEK WORDS

1. "devils" — δαιμόνια (*daimonia*): evil spirits; demons; devils; the ancient world believed demons populated the lower regions of the air and that spirits were the primary cause of disasters and suffering in the earth; could depict a person deemed mentally sick or insane; in New Testament writings, δαιμόνια (*daimonia*) often depicts those

oppressed by evil spirits as having mental or physical infirmities that are spirit-inflicted

2. "subject" — ὑποτάσσω (*hupotasso*): used militarily to depict a soldier who falls in line when a commander gives an order; one submitted to authority

3. "beheld" — θεωρέω (*theoreo*): to gaze at; to look upon; the root from which we get the word "theater"

4. "power" — ἐξουσία (*exousia*): authority; denotes one who has received delegated power

5. "tread" — πατέω (*pateo*): to walk on; to trample, to crush; to advance by setting the foot upon

6. "serpents" — ὄφις (*ophis*): a serpent; snake; pictures the devil or Satan

7. "scorpions" — σκορπίος (*skorpios*): a scorpion; a creature with a venomous sting

8. "over" — ἐπὶ (*epi*): over; denotes a position of advantage and superiority

9. "power" — δύναμις (*dunamis*): power; dynamic power; superhuman power; depicts the full force of an advancing army

10. "enemy" — ἐχθρός (*echthros*): an irreconcilable hostility; pictures an enemy; someone who is openly hostile; one with a deep-seated hatred; one who is bent on inflicting harm

11. "demons" — δαιμόνιον (*daimonion*): evil spirits; demons; devils; the ancient world believed demons populated the lower regions of the air and that spirits were the primary cause of disasters and suffering in the earth; could depict a person deemed mentally sick or insane; in New Testament writings, δαιμόνια (*daimonia*) often depicts those oppressed by evil spirits as having mental or physical infirmities that are spirit-inflicted. They are highly organized under Satan as rulers, authorities, powers, and spiritual forces of evil.

SYNOPSIS

The five lessons in this study on *What the New Testament Tells Us About Demons* will focus on the following topics:

- The Demoniac of Gadara
- Demonic Infestations
- Demonic Terror, Destruction, and Strength

- Demonic Ferociousness, Self-Destruction, and Fits
- Demonic Submission to Jesus

The emphasis of this lesson:

Demons are real, but we have been given all authority over them in the name of Jesus.

Located on the eastern shore of the Sea of Galilee are the ruins of a large monastery built in the Fifth Century. It is believed to be the largest one constructed in the land of Israel. Its location is in the vicinity of the Gadarenes, and it marks the place where a mighty miracle occurred. It is here where Jesus met two demon-possessed men living among the tombs. With great authority and power, Christ delivered them from the enemy's grasp, and He is still setting people free from demons today.

Jesus Recognized the Reality of Demons

The Bible says that after Jesus had selected and sent out 70 disciples to minister in His name, "…the seventy returned again with joy, saying, Lord, even the devils are subject unto us through thy name" (Luke 10:17). The word "devils" here is the Greek word *daimonia*, and it describes *evil spirits, demons,* or *devils.* The ancient world believed demons populated the lower regions of the air and that spirits were the primary cause of disasters and suffering in the earth. The word *daimonia* can also depict *a person deemed mentally sick or insane.* In New Testament writings, *daimonia* often portrayed those oppressed by evil spirits as having mental or physical infirmities that were spirit-inflicted.

Also notice the word "subject" in this passage. It is the Greek word *hupotasso*, and it is used militarily to depict *a soldier who falls in line when a commander gives an order*, or *one submitted to authority.* This word lets us know that demon spirits recognize spiritual authority. The 70 disciples Jesus sent out came to realize that even demons will fall in line when they spoke a commanding word through the name of Jesus.

In response to the 70, Jesus said, "…I beheld Satan as lightning fall from heaven" (Luke 10:18). The word "beheld" is the Greek word *theoreo*, which means *to gaze at; to look upon.* It is the root from which we get the word "theater." When Satan was kicked out of Heaven, Jesus was right there watching it take place like a spectator who sits in a theater and watches every act of a play or musical performance. Like a flash of lightning,

Lucifer was reduced to nothing and hurled out of God's presence — forever. The details of this event are found in Isaiah 14:12-15 and Ezekiel 28:12-19.

The Lord Has Given You Authority and Power Over the Enemy

Jesus went on to say, "Behold, I give unto you power to tread on serpents and scorpions, and over all the power of the enemy; and nothing shall by any means hurt you" (Luke 10:19). In this verse, the word "behold" in the Greek would be better translated as, "Wow! What I'm about to tell you is so amazing! I'm nearly speechless as I describe it."

Jesus then said He has given us "power" — the Greek word *exousia*, which means *authority*. It denotes *one who has received delegated power*. Thus, when we stand against the enemy and his demonic forces, we are not operating in our own ability, or in our own authority and power. We are operating in the power and authority of Jesus Christ. It is His promised gift to you and to every believer.

Through Jesus, we can "tread on serpents and scorpions." The word "tread" is the Greek word *pateo*, and it means *to walk on; to trample, crush, or advance by setting the foot upon*. The enemy will always try to block your forward progress. In order for you to advance, you will have to purposefully trample him under your feet.

Jesus has given you delegated authority to tread upon "serpents and scorpions." The word "serpents" in Greek is *ophis*, and it means *serpent* or *snake*. The New Testament writers use this word to represent *the devil or Satan*. Every time he tries to snake his way into your life, you are to trample him under your feet by speaking the Word of God against him and using your God-given authority in Christ's name.

We also have authority over "scorpions." This is the Greek word *skorpios*, which means *a scorpion; a creature with a venomous sting*. The use of this word informs us that sometimes the devil tries to create "stinging" situations to stun and stop us from fulfilling God's plan. If that happens, know that Jesus has given you the authority and power to trample and crush him under your feet.

He said in Luke 10:19 that you have authority "over all the power of the enemy." The word "over" is the Greek word *epi*, which denotes *a position of advantage and superiority.* The word "power" is the Greek word *dunamis*, which means *power; dynamic power; superhuman power.* Technically, it depicts *the full force of an advancing army.*

Last is the word "enemy," which is the Greek word *echthros*, and it describes *an irreconcilable hostility.* It pictures *an enemy; someone who is openly hostile; one with a deep-seated hatred; one who is bent on inflicting harm.* This word describes explicitly what the devil desires to do to everyone.

Essentially, Jesus said, "When the devil launches an all-out attack against you, don't worry or fret. I have given you *authority and the advantageous, superior position over all the hostile forces and advancing army of the enemy that come against you to try to inflict harm.*" First John 4:4 confirms this truth, declaring, "...Greater is he that is in you, than he that is in the world." There is no need to fear demons; you have been given delegated authority over them by Jesus Himself, and they will fall in line when you speak the command in His name.

The Man Who Lived Among the Tombs

Jesus performed many miracles throughout the land of Israel, especially in Galilee. One particular miracle was done in the vicinity of the Gadarenes, which is located just east of the Sea of Galilee. It was there that Christ demonstrated His power over demons. Mark 5:1 and 2 says, "And they came over unto the other side of the sea, into the country of the Gadarenes. And when he was come out of the ship, immediately there met him out of the tombs a man with an unclean spirit."

Interestingly, the gospel of Matthew also records this event, but it notes that there were *two* demon-possessed men (*see* Matthew 8:28). Although it seems to be contradictory, it isn't. Matthew gives us a broader scope of what took place, and Mark zeros in on the man who was more severely possessed. According to Mark's gospel, this man was living in a graveyard, which indicates that he had death on his mind constantly.

This demonized man lived in indescribable misery. Mark 5:3-5 tells us that time and time again, he had been locked in chains that had been secured around his feet and wrists, but no one could keep him bound. Day and night he cried aloud and tried to take his own life by cutting himself with stones, but he was unsuccessful. The enemy abused him and used him to terrorize the entire region. But when Jesus came, he was miraculously set free!

What the Bible Tells Us About Demons

The Bible reveals some specific things about demons that you need to know.

- **Demons are highly organized under Satan's authority.** There are principalities, powers, rulers of the darkness of this world, and spiritual wickedness in high places (*see* Ephesians 6:12).

- **Demons have the ability to demonize people** (*see* Luke 8:30). Although the words "demon possession" are often used by Christians today and appear in many modern translations of Scripture, the original Greek does not say that. It says that people were *demonized*.

- **Demons are able to appear to human beings** (*see* Job 4:15).

- **Demons can be driven out of a demonized person.** Scripture explicitly teaches that we have authority to cast them out. However, if the person that is set free from a demon and is not saved, the demon that was cast out of him or her will come back and bring seven more demons with him; and the person's latter condition will be worse than at the beginning (*see* Matthew 12:43-45).

- **Demons are seducing in nature, leading people into error** (*see* 1 Timothy 4:1).

- **Demons frequent places where paganism, idol worship, and occult activity occur.** This is a fact mentioned by the apostle Paul in First Corinthians 10:20 and 21.

- **Demons can inhabit animals** (*see* Matthew 8:31; Mark 5:11-13; Luke 8:32,33).

- **Demons will torture people during the Great Tribulation.** The Bible says that when they are released on the earth during this time, they will appear as locusts (*see* Revelation 9:1-7).

- **Demons will eventually be eternally incarcerated by God in a prison called the Abyss.** They will be locked up forever (*see* Revelation 20:10).

In this series, we will explore nine specific things you need to know about demons. These include:

- Demonic Infestations
- Demonic Terror
- Demonic Destruction
- Demonic Strength
- Demonic Ferociousness
- Demonic Self-Destruction
- Demonic Fits
- Demonic Stubbornness
- Demonic Submission to Jesus

Regardless of what demons can do and how much of a nuisance they can be, they are no match for Jesus. And in His name you have been given all power and authority over the enemy.

STUDY QUESTIONS

**Study to shew thyself approved unto God, a workman that
needeth not to be ashamed, rightly dividing the word of truth.
— 2 Timothy 2:15**

1. Prior to this lesson, what was your understanding and thoughts about the devil and demons?

2. What new insights have you gained so far, and how has your perspective on the topic changed?

3. The power and authority we have over the enemy and his demonic forces is all a result of the mighty name of Jesus. God the Father gave Christ His name. Carefully read Philippians 2:6-11 and identify what will eventually happen "at the name of Jesus" and why God has given Him this matchless honor.

PRACTICAL APPLICATION

**But be ye doers of the word, and not hearers only,
deceiving your own selves.
— James 1:22**

1. Understanding the supreme authority of Jesus Christ over all powers is the first step in understanding your authority in Him. Carefully

read Colossians 1:15-20; 2:9,10 and ask the Holy Spirit to give you a deeper revelation of His authority.

2. The apostle Paul also talked about the supremacy of Christ in Ephesians 1:17-23. Slowly read through these verses and describe what the Holy Spirit is showing you about Christ's authority and *your* authority in Him (also *consider* Ephesians 2:4-6; Luke 10:19).

TOPIC

Demonic Infestations

SCRIPTURES

1. **Luke 10:19** — Behold, I give unto you power to tread on serpents and scorpions, and over all the power of the enemy....

2. **1 John 4:4** — Ye are of God, little children, and have overcome them: because greater is he that is in you, than he that is in the world.

3. **Mark 5:1-9** — And they came over unto the other side of the sea, into the country of the Gadarenes. And when he was come out of the ship, immediately there met him out of the tombs a man with an unclean spirit. Who had his dwelling among the tombs; and no man could bind him, no, not with chains. Because that he had been often bound with fetters and chains, and the chains had been plucked asunder by him, and the fetters broken in pieces: neither could any man tame him. And always, night and day, he was in the mountains, and in the tombs, crying, and cutting himself with stones. But when he saw Jesus afar off, he ran and worshipped him. And cried with a loud voice, and said, What have I to do with thee, Jesus, thou Son of the most high God? I adjure thee by God, that thou torment me not. For he said unto him, Come out of the man, thou unclean spirit. And he asked him, What is thy name? And he answered, saying, My name is Legion: for we are many.

4. **Colossians 2:9,10** — For in him dwelleth all the fulness of the Godhead bodily. And ye are complete in him, which is the head of all principality and power.

GREEK WORDS

1. "subject" — ὑποτάσσω (*hupotasso*): used militarily to depict a soldier who falls in line when a commander gives an order; one submitted to authority

2. "beheld" — θεωρέω (*theoreo*): to gaze at; to look upon; the root from which we get the word "theater"

3. "power" — ἐξουσία (*exousia*): authority; denotes one who has received delegated power

4. "tread" — πατέω (*pateo*): to walk on; to trample, to crush; to advance by setting the foot upon

5. "serpents" — ὄφις (*ophis*): a serpent; snake; pictures the devil or Satan

6. "scorpions" — σκορπίος (*skorpios*): a scorpion; a creature with a venomous sting

7. "over" — ἐπὶ (*epi*): over; denotes a position of advantage and superiority

8. "power" — δύναμις (*dunamis*): power; dynamic power; superhuman power; depicts the full force of an advancing army

9. "enemy" — ἐχθρός (*echthros*): an irreconcilable hostility; pictures an enemy; someone who is openly hostile; one with a deep-seated hatred; one who is bent on inflicting harm

10. "demons" — δαιμόνιον (*daimonion*): evil spirits; demons; devils; the ancient world believed demons populated the lower regions of the air and that spirits were the primary cause of disasters and suffering in the earth; could depict a person deemed mentally sick or insane; in New Testament writings, δαιμόνια (*daimonia*) often depicts those oppressed by evil spirits as having mental or physical infirmities that are spirit-inflicted; they are highly organized under Satan as rulers, authorities, powers, and spiritual forces of evil

11. "immediately" — εὐθὺς (*euthus*): without delay; immediately

12. "met" — ὑπαντάω (*hupantao*): to meet face to face; used militarily to denote a hostile meeting

13. "out" — ἐκ (*out*): out; root word from which we get the word "exit"

14. "tombs" — μνῆμα (*mnema*): graves; tombs; tombstones

15. "with an unclean spirit" — ἐν πνεύματι ἀκαθάρτῳ (*en pneumati akatharto*): in the grip of an unclean spirit; in the control of an unclean spirit

16. "unclean" — **ἀκάθαρτος** (*akathartos*): unclean, impure, filthy, lewd, or foul

17. "said" — **ἔλεγεν** (*elegen*): the Greek tense means, "He kept on saying…"

18. "legion" — **Λεγιὼν** (*Legion*): a military term that denoted at least 6,000 Roman soldiers

19. "we are many" — **πολλοί ἐσμεν** (*polloi esmen*): we are many in number; we are a multitude; we are a vast number

SYNOPSIS

Gadara was the capital of the Roman province of Peraea, and it was located about six miles east of the Sea of Galilee. Today the ruins of a Fifth Century monastery commemorating Jesus' miracle deliverance of the demoniacs stand in this location. Matthew 8:28 says when Jesus arrived, "…There met him two possessed with devils, coming out of the tombs, exceeding fierce, so that no one might pass by that way." For years, these two demonized men terrorized this entire region, leaving people paralyzed in fear. But Jesus was not afraid. He took the authority given to Him by the Father and cast the demons out of these men, thereby liberating the whole region from fear.

The emphasis of this lesson:

The demoniacs of Gadara are a vivid picture of demonic infestation. Their deliverance illustrates the matchless power and authority of Jesus, as well as the enormity of our spiritual capacity in Him.

The Foundation of Our Authority Over Demons

In Luke 10:19, Jesus spoke to His disciples — and to us — saying, "Behold, I give unto you power to tread on serpents and scorpions, and over all the power of the enemy: any nothing shall by any means hurt you." In our last lesson, we learned that the word "behold" in Greek actually means, "Wow! This is amazing!" Essentially, Jesus was saying, "Wow! What I'm about to tell you is so spectacular, it nearly leaves Me speechless."

We also saw that the first mention of the word "power" here is the Greek word *exousia*, which means *authority*. It denotes *one who has received delegated power.* The authority you have over the enemy is not willpower or any ability within yourself. It is authority given to you from Jesus Christ, and you operate in that authority through His mighty name.

He said you are to "tread on serpents and scorpions." The word "tread" is the Greek word *pateo*, and it means *to walk on; to trample or crush; to advance by setting the foot upon.* Realize that Satan and his forces will try to trip you up and hinder your advancement. But just keep putting one foot in front of the other and "tread" upon their heads — trample and crush them as you move forward in faith.

"Serpents" is the Greek word *ophis*, and it describes a *serpent* or *snake.* In the New Testament, it pictures *the devil* or *Satan himself.* The word "scorpions" is the Greek words *skorpios*, which denotes *a scorpion; a creature with a venomous sting.* This puts you on notice that just as a scorpion will hide in the rocks along the roadway, the enemy will hide and attempt to sabotage your journey with "stinging" situations. But Jesus doesn't want you to be moved by the threat of serpents or scorpions. He has given you delegated authority to *tread* on them.

In Luke 10:19 He declared that you have authority "over all the power of the enemy." The word "over" in this verse is the Greek word *epi*, which means *upon* or *over*, and it denotes *a position of advantage and superiority.* This means in Christ, you have been given a superior position over all the "power" of the enemy.

This second use of the word "power" is the Greek word *dunamis*, and it describes *power; dynamic power; superhuman power.* It depicts *the full force of an advancing army.* When it appears as though the devil has unleashed the full force of his army to advance against you, rest assured it is no match for the authority Jesus has given you.

The word "enemy" in verse 19 is the Greek word *echthros*, and it pictures *an enemy; someone who is openly hostile; one with a deep-seated hatred and irreconcilable hostility; one who is bent on inflicting harm.* This is exactly what the devil and his demons desire to do to you and to all mankind. Nevertheless, you have been given authority (*exousia*) over (*epi*) the enemy — you have a position of victory and superiority in Christ Jesus.

What We Know About Demons From Scripture

The four gospels and the epistles reveal many things about demons:

1. **Demons scream** (*see* Mark 1:23,26; 3:11; 5:7; 9:26; Luke 4:33; 8:28; Acts 8:7).

2. **Demons cry out.** The words "cry out" are from the Greek word *anakradzo*, and it is used repeatedly in Scripture. It describes *an endless, blood-curdling scream.* This scream is usually in response to demons encountering the power of Jesus (*see* Mark 1:23; Luke 4:33; 8:28).

3. **Demons can be panicked or spooked** (*see* Matthew 8:29; Mark 1:24; Mark 5:7; Luke 8:28).

4. **Demons talk or converse.** In fact, they talk so much that many times Jesus commanded them to be silent (*see* Mark 1:34; 5:9; Luke 4:41; Act 19:15).

5. **Demons have intelligence.** They can know things about people (*see* Mark 5:7; Acts 19:15).

6. **Demons are unclean.** Jesus often called them "unclean" spirits. The word "unclean" describes *something filthy, foul, dirty, and lewd* (*see* Matthew 12:43; 15:22; Mark 1:23,26; 3:20; 5:2; 5:8; 9:25; Luke 4:33; 8:29; 9:42; 11:24).

7. **Demons are violent.** They tend to do violent things if no one takes authority over them and restricts them (*see* Matthew 17:14-18; Mark 5:13; 9:14-29; Luke 9:37-42; Acts 19:16).

8. **Demons tend to cause terror** (*see* Matthew 8:28; Acts 19:16).

9. **Demons can be incredibly strong.** They will exhibit superhuman strength unless restricted (*see* Mark 5:4; Luke 8:29; Acts 19:16).

10. **Demons can cause physical impairments** (*see* Matthew 9:33; 12:22-30; Mark 3:20-27; Luke 11:14-23).

11. **Demons can cause suicidal tendencies** (*see* Mark 5:5).

12. **Demons can inhabit animals.** In Gadara, Jesus sent the demons into a herd of pigs (*see* Matthew 8:31; Mark 5:11-13; Luke 8:32,33).

13. **Demons can operate through occult activities** (*see* Matthew 17:15).

14. **Demons can be religious.** They don't always act like the devil (*see* Mark 1:24; 5:7; Luke 8:28).

15. **Demons believe.** They know who Jesus is more than us (*see* James 2:19).

16. **Demons can beg and pray.** This is especially true when they are put under pressure; they beg and plead to be released (*see* Matthew 8:31; Mark 5:7,10,12; Luke 8:31-32).

17. **Demons recognize authority.** When you operate in the authority of Christ, they recognize it (*see* Mark 1:27; Luke 4:36; Acts 19:15).
18. **Demons can be resisted.** When you submit to God and resist the enemy, he will flee (*see* James 4:7).
19. **Demons submit to the name and authority of Jesus Christ** (*see* Mark 1:27; Luke 4:36; Acts 19:15).

Jesus Was Met By a Demoniac in Gadara — the Most Severely Affected of the Two Demonized Men

The biblical account of the demoniac who was set free from Satan's power is not a fairytale. It is an event that actually took place near the eastern shore of the Sea of Galilee. Mark retells the story saying, "And they [Jesus and His disciples] came over unto the other side of the sea, into the country of the Gadarenes. And when he was come out of the ship, immediately there met him out of the tombs a man with an unclean spirit" (Mark 5:1,2).

First, notice the word "immediately" — the Greek word *euthus*, meaning *without delay; immediately*. The moment Jesus stepped out of the boat, He was confronted by this demonized man. The Bible says the man "met" Him. The word "met" in Greek is the word *hupantao*, which means *to meet face-to-face*. It is used militarily to denote *a hostile meeting*. The demons in this man were ready to fight. Jesus was invading their territory, and they didn't want to lose an inch of it.

This man came from "out of the tombs." The word "out" is the Greek word *ek*; it is *the root term from where we get the word "exit."* And the word "tombs" is the Greek word *mnema*, which means *graves; tombs; tombstones*. When Jesus set foot on the soil of the Gadarenes, the demoniac *exited* the city cemetery and came straight toward Jesus. This is confirmed in Luke 8:27, which states that the demon-possessed man who lived "in the tombs" came from "out of the city."

The fact that he was living "among" or "in" the tombs tells us he lived surrounded by death. It was all around him and constantly on his mind. The demons that inhabited him had driven him to a place of death, and eventually they would try to drive him to make multiple attempts of suicide.

The Man Had an Unclean Spirit

Looking at Mark 5:2 again, it says that the man living among the tombs was "with an unclean spirit." The phrase "with an unclean spirit" in Greek is *en pneumati akatharto*, which means *in the grip of an unclean spirit* or *in the control of an unclean spirit*. Therefore, this man didn't have an unclean spirit; the unclean spirit had him. He was literally in the grip and control of an unclean spirit.

The word "unclean" is the Greek word *akathartos*, and it means *unclean, impure, filthy, lewd, or foul*. Unclean spirits are so filthy and impure that they will live anywhere — even among the death and decay of a graveyard.

The Bible goes on to say, "...No man could bind him, no, not with chains. Because that he had been often bound with fetters and chains, and the chains had been plucked asunder by him, and the fetters broken in pieces: neither could any man tame him. And always, night and day, he was in the mountains, and in the tombs, crying, and cutting himself with stones. But when he saw Jesus afar off, he ran and worshipped him" (Mark 5:3-6).

Jesus Took Authority Over the Demons

As the man lay upon the ground worshiping Jesus, the Scripture says the demon spirit "cried with a loud voice, and said, What have I to do with thee, Jesus, thou Son of the most high God? I adjure thee by God, that thou torment me not" (Mark 5:7). Verse 8 states that Jesus "...said unto him, Come out of the man, thou unclean spirit."

It's interesting to note that the Greek tense in this verse actually indicates that Jesus *kept saying over and over and over*, "Come out of him, come out of him, come out of him." Apparently, the demons were initially resistant to surrender and to obey Jesus' command.

This interaction between Christ and the unclean spirit was quite unusual. Usually, when the Lord cast demons out of someone, He did it with a single command. Just one word from the lips of the Master, and the demons vacated. But when we come to this account in Mark 5 (also recorded in Matthew 8:28-34 and Luke 8:26-39), we see that the demons wouldn't budge at first.

Then in Mark 5:9, Jesus asked, "What is thy name?" The rest of that verse reads, "...And he answered, saying, My name is Legion: for we are many."

Jesus wanted to know why the unclean spirit wouldn't budge, so He asked its name. "Legion," the demon snarled back, "for we are many." The word "legion" is the Greek word *legion*, which is *a military term that denoted at least 6,000 Roman soldiers*. By using the word "legion," the unclean spirit was saying, "You are talking to me, but there are 6,000 of us inside this man," which brings us to the phrase "we are many." This is the Greek phrase *polloi esmen*, and it means *we are many in number; we are a multitude; we are a vast number*.

The Immensity of Our Spiritual Capacity

This one man who was housing 6,000 demons gives us a vivid picture of a demonic *infestation*. It also reveals the enormity of each person's spiritual capacity, which is actually much larger than we realize. For example, if this one man could hold 6,000 demons, how much of God's Spirit can one man hold?

Colossians 2:9 says, "For in him [Jesus] dwelleth all the fulness of the Godhead bodily." When Jesus Christ walked the earth, He contained the fullness of the Godhead in His physical form. Even now as He is seated at the right hand of God, He is filled through and through with all that God is.

How about you? How much of God's Spirit can *you* hold? Colossians 2:10 (*AMPC*) gives the answer. It says, "And you are in Him, made full and having come to the fullness of life [in Christ you too are filled with the Godhead — Father, Son and Holy Spirit — and reach full spiritual stature]...."

Positionally — in Christ — you have the right to be filled with the exact same fullness of God that Jesus received. Every day, take time to pray and ask the Holy Spirit of God to fill you more and more with the fullness of who He is. You will be amazed at how He answers your request!

STUDY QUESTIONS

> Study to shew thyself approved unto God, a workman that
> needeth not to be ashamed, rightly dividing the word of truth.
> — 2 Timothy 2:15

In this lesson, Rick listed many characteristics about demons that are mentioned in the four gospels and the epistles. Take a few moments to look back through the list.

1. Which attributes were you unaware of and most surprised to learn about? Why?
2. Look up the verses connected with the trait that is most intriguing to you and write what the Holy Spirit shows you.

PRACTICAL APPLICATION

> But be ye doers of the word, and not hearers only,
> deceiving your own selves.
> —James 1:22

The fact that one man could be filled with 6,000 demonic spirits illustrates the enormity of our spiritual capacity. Take a few moments to meditate on Colossians 2:9,10 (*AMPC*): "For in Him the whole fullness of Deity (the Godhead) continues to dwell in bodily form [giving complete expression of the divine nature]. And you are in Him, made full and having come to the fullness of life [in Christ you too are filled with the Godhead — Father, Son and Holy Spirit — and reach full spiritual stature]...."

1. What does this passage say to you about your personal *spiritual capacity*?
2. Be honest. What are you more "full" of — the things of this world or the Spirit of God? How do you think your family and close friends would answer this question for you?
3. What adjustments do you know in your heart you need to make in order to take in and experience more of the fullness of God?

TOPIC
Demonic Terror, Destruction, and Strength

SCRIPTURES

1. **Luke 10:19** — Behold, I give unto you power to tread on serpents and scorpions, and over all the power of the enemy....

2. **Mark 5:1-5** — And they came over unto the other side of the sea, into the country of the Gadarenes. And when he was come out of the ship, immediately there met him out of the tombs a man with an unclean spirit. Who had his dwelling among the tombs; and no man could bind him, no, not with chains. Because that he had been often bound with fetters and chains, and the chains had been plucked asunder by him, and the fetters broken in pieces: neither could any man tame him. And always, night and day, he was in the mountains, and in the tombs, crying, and cutting himself with stones.

3. **Matthew 8:28** — And when he was come to the other side into the country of the Gergesenes, there met him two possessed with devils, coming out of the tombs, exceeding fierce, so that no man might pass by that way.

GREEK WORDS

1. "power" — ἐξουσία (*exousia*): authority; denotes one who has received delegated power

2. "tread" — πατέω (*pateo*): to walk on; to trample, to crush; to advance by setting the foot upon

3. "over" — ἐπὶ (*epi*): over; denotes a position of advantage and superiority

4. "immediately" — εὐθὺς (*euthus*): without delay; immediately

5. "met" — ὑπαντάω (*hupantao*): to meet face to face; used militarily to denote a hostile meeting

6. "tombs" — μνῆμα (*mnema*): graves; tombs; tombstones

7. "with an unclean spirit" — ἐν πνεύματι ἀκαθάρτῳ (*en pneumati akatharto*): in the grip of an unclean spirit; in the control of an unclean spirit

8. "unclean" — ἀκάθαρτος (*akathartos*): unclean, impure, filthy, lewd, or foul

9. "bind" — δέω (*deo*): to bind, tie up, restrict, imprison, or put in chains

10. "chains" — ἅλυσις (*halusis*): chains or handcuffs for the hands or wrists

11. "fetters" — πέδη (*pede*): shackles on the feet; foot chains

12. "plucked asunder" — διασπάω (*diaspao*): to tear in half; to sever; to tear to pieces

13. "broken in pieces" — συντρίβω (*suntribo*): to crush, as in crushing bones or grapes; to smash

14. "tame" — δαμάζω (*damadzo*): to domesticate, to subdue, or to bring under control; used to describe animal trainers who were experts at capturing and domesticating the wildest and most ferocious beasts, such as lions, tigers, and bears; these animals had a tendency to maul or kill a person, but skilled trainers were able to tame the wildest animals and domesticate them

15. "always, night and day" — διὰ παντὸς νυκτὸς καὶ ἡμέρας (*dia pantos nuktos kai hemeras*): constantly, throughout nighttime and daytime; perpetually, when it is dark and when it is light

16. "crying" — κράζω (*kradzo*): pictures an agonizing scream

17. "cutting" — κατακόπτω (*katakopto*): to cut downward; to gash downward; to mutilate

18. "exceedingly fierce" — χαλεπός (*chalepos*): pictures something dangerous, risky, or hurtful; something that is wounding; used in various pieces of literature to depict wild, vicious, uncontrollable animals that are unpredictable and dangerous; depicts a deadly menace; thus, it can be used to denote anything that is treacherous or potentially hurtful; carries the idea of an action, place, person, or thing that is harsh, harmful, and filled with high risk

SYNOPSIS

The remains of a Byzantine chapel built in the Fifth Century can be found today near the eastern shore of the Sea of Galilee. It was constructed to commemorate Jesus' powerful display of authority over a legion of demons which had taken up residence in a man from the country of the Gadarenes. Tormented continually, this man had been driven by Satan to the brink of total annihilation. When Jesus showed up, He set him free and totally restored his life. Matthew, Mark, and Luke — also known as the Synoptic Gospels — all record this powerful story from Jesus' ministry.

The emphasis of this lesson:

The demonized man from Gadara displayed supernatural strength, ripping in two the metal restraints around his arms and pulverizing the chains around his feet. Yet his feats of terror and destruction didn't cause Jesus to deviate from His mission of freedom.

Our foundational verse for this series is Luke 10:19. Here Jesus said, "Behold, I give unto you power to tread on serpents and scorpions, and over all the power of the enemy; and nothing shall by any means hurt you." From this scripture, we see that Jesus has given us "power," which is the Greek word *exousia*, and it means *authority*. You have authority to "tread" on serpents and scorpions.

We learned that the word "tread" is the Greek word *pateo*, and it means *to walk on; to trample; to crush; to advance by setting the foot upon*. Jesus was saying, "If the devil tries to get in your way, don't stop or retreat. Keep moving forward in faith. I have given you authority over all the power of the enemy." The word "over" is the Greek word *epi*, which means *over* and *denotes a position of advantage and superiority*. As a believer, you are in Christ and have a superior position over all the "power" the enemy possesses.

This second inclusion of the word "power" is different than the first. It is the Greek word *dunamis* — the same word that describes *the full force of an advancing Roman army*. By using this word, Jesus was saying, "Even if the devil sends his hordes of hell against you with all the might they can muster, they are no match for the authority I have given you."

Jesus Encountered the Demoniac Face-to-Face

Mark chapter 5 offers a detailed account of the deliverance of the demoniac by the hands of Jesus. Verses 1 and 2 read, "And they came over unto the other side of the sea, into the country of the Gadarenes. And when he was come out of the ship, immediately there met him out of the tombs a man with an unclean spirit."

In this verse, the word "immediately" is the Greek word *euthus*, which means *without delay; immediately.* The word "met" is the Greek word *hupantao*, which was *a term used militarily to denote a hostile meeting*, or *an aggressive face-to-face encounter.* Thus, the unclean spirit in this man *immediately* came out to challenge Jesus just as it had challenged everyone else who passed that way.

The Bible says he came from "out of the tombs." The word "out" is the Greek word *ek*; it is where we get the word "exit." This man literally *exited* the "tombs" and darted toward Jesus. The word "tombs" in Greek is *mnema*, and it describes *graves; tombs; tombstones.* This is the first of three mentions of the man living among the "tombs."

Verse 2 also tells us that the man was "with an unclean spirit," which in Greek means *in the grip of an unclean spirit* or *in the control of an unclean spirit.* Hence, this man didn't just have an unclean spirit; the unclean spirit had total control of this man. The word "unclean" is the Greek word *akathartos*, and it describes *something unclean, impure, filthy, lewd, or foul.* This is the word repeatedly used throughout the New Testament to describe evil spirits.

The Man Had Often Been Bound With Chains and Fetters

In Mark 5:3, we are told for a second time that this man "had his dwelling among the tombs." The word "dwelling" means *to take up residence*, which is exactly what he did. He was living "among" the tombs. The word "among" is the Greek word *en*, which means he was literally *living in the midst of the graves.* Interestingly, we will see in the coming lessons that this man didn't always live among the tombs; he once lived in a house.

Verse 3 goes on to say, "…No man could bind him, no not with chains." The words "no man" in Greek literally mean *no one — no, not a single one.* This indicates that many had attempted to bind him, but no one "could" do it. The word "could" in Greek means *to be able to muster strength or power.* Thus, not one single person was able to muster enough strength to effectively "bind" this man. The word "bind" is the Greek word *deo*, which means *to bind, tie up, restrict, imprison, or put in chains.* And the word "chains" in Greek is the word *halusis*, and it describes *chains or handcuffs for the hands or wrists.*

Not only had this man's hands been bound, but also his feet. Mark 5:4 says, "...He had been often bound with fetters and chains...." The word "fetters" is the Greek word *pedes*, and it comes from the word *podos*, which is the word for *feet*. Thus the word *pedes* refers to *shackles on the feet; foot chains*.

It's interesting to note that the word "chains" (*halusis*) doesn't describe the type of chains you might imagine. These restraints were a solid piece of metal wrapped around both arms in such a way that it was extremely difficult to use your hands to exert strength in order to break free.

They Were 'Plucked Asunder' and 'Broken in Pieces'

The Bible says this man was bound in chains and fetters "often," which literally means *recurrently* or *frequently*. Again and again and again, his arms and feet had been bound with metal restraints, but no man could keep him confined. Verse 4 goes on to say, "...The chains had been plucked asunder by him, and the fetters broken in pieces...."

The phrase "plucked asunder" is the Greek word *diaspao*, which means *to tear in half; to sever; to tear to pieces*. This man was so demonically energized that he was able to rip the metal restraints that were around his arms to shreds.

He did similarly to the fetters around his feet. The phrase "broken in pieces" is the well-known Greek word *suntribo*, which means *to crush, as in crushing bones or the crushing of grapes to produce wine; to smash*. By using this word, the Holy Spirit is telling us that this demoniac was so empowered by demons that he would bang together the metal straps around his legs and ankles, grinding them so ferociously that they were reduced to dust.

No Man Could 'Tame' Him

Not only could the demoniac not be bound by chains or fetters, the Bible also says, "...Neither could any man tame him" (Mark 5:4). The word "tame" is the Greek term *damadzo*, which means *to domesticate, to subdue, or to bring under control*. This word was used to describe *animal trainers who were experts at capturing and domesticating the wildest and most ferocious beasts, such as lions, tigers, and bears*. These animals had a tendency to maul or kill a person, but skilled trainers were able to take the wildest animals and domesticate them.

In this case, no one — not even highly skilled animal trainers — were able to capture, subdue, domesticate, or bring this demonized man under control. Even the experts at incarcerating wild beasts were unable to bind this man. Whenever they put chains around his arms and hands, he was able to rip them in two. When they fastened shackles around his feet, he beat them into dust.

You may know someone in a situation that seems to be totally out of control. *Can anyone help them?* you might be asking yourself. *They've tried medication, counseling, and many other things, but nothing has worked.* God wants to remind you that what is impossible with man is possible with Him (*see* Matthew 19:26). As Jesus successfully delivered the demoniac, He can successfully deliver anyone. Don't give up hope!

Demonization Produced Suicidal Tendencies

Mark 5:5 continues to reveal this man's condition of misery. It says, "And always, night and day, he was in the mountains, and in the tombs, crying, and cutting himself with stones." Notice the phrase "always, night and day." In Greek, it means *constantly, throughout nighttime and daytime; perpetually, when it is dark and when it is light.* Wherever this man went — in the mountains are among the tombs, all day and all night — he couldn't escape the torment of the demons.

Scripture says he was "crying" — the Greek word *kradzo*. It pictures *an agonizing scream.* And in addition to yelling, he was also "cutting" himself. The word "cutting" is the Greek word *katakopto*, which means *to cut downward; to gash downward; to mutilate.* Clearly, this man was trying to commit suicide, and it was the demons living inside him that were driving him to it.

Remember, he was living "among the tombs." He was surrounded by death; it was constantly before his eyes and constantly on his mind. The truth is, he was closer to death than he was to life, and it's no wonder he repeatedly attempted to take his own life. The mental, emotional, and spiritual torture he was experiencing was horrific.

No one could help him. Wild animal tamers couldn't bind him or domesticate him, and religious people couldn't set him free from his agony. Some scholars believe this man may have been trying to liberate himself from the demon spirits by trying to end his life. He may have thought that his only hope of freedom was through death. But God had other plans.

Were There *One* or *Two* Demonized Men?

As noted earlier, the story of Jesus delivering the demoniac is also recorded in Matthew 8. What's interesting about Matthew's account is that he says there were not one, but *two* men being held captive by demons. Matthew 8:28 says, "And when he [Jesus] was come to the other side into the country of the Gergesenes, there met him two possessed with devils, coming out of the tombs, exceeding fierce, so that no man might pass by that way."

Notice the Bible says these two demonized men were "exceedingly fierce." This is the Greek word *chalepos*, and it pictures *something dangerous, risky, or hurtful; something that is wounding.* The word *chalepos* is used in various pieces of literature to depict *wild, vicious, uncontrollable animals that are unpredictable and dangerous.* Thus, it can be used to denote *anything that is treacherous or potentially hurtful.* It carries the idea of *an action, place, person, or thing that is harsh, harmful, and filled with high risk.*

Therefore, when the Bible says these two men came out of the tombs "exceedingly fierce," it indicates that they created an extremely dangerous and treacherous situation for all those passing by. Yet Jesus was unfazed. He had authority over the demons and exercised it fully. And He has given you His authority to tread upon all the power of the enemy as well (*see* Luke 10:19).

If you're born again, you are in Christ, and the demons recognize your voice as the voice of Jesus. So open your mouth and take authority over every filthy, foul spirit that has come against you and your family. In the name of Jesus, put the devil in his place and walk in your God-given freedom.

STUDY QUESTIONS

> Study to shew thyself approved unto God, a workman that needeth
> not to be ashamed, rightly dividing the word of truth.
> — 2 Timothy 2:15

Despite the enemy's terrorizing threats and appearance, Jesus has given you His authority to live boldly and overcome all of Satan's power. Proverbs 28:1 declares, "…The righteous are bold as a lion."

1. According to Hebrews 4:15,16 and Hebrews 10:16-23, for what reasons should you walk boldly?

2. From where does your strength to stand against the enemy come? (*See* Psalm 27; Psalm 28:8; 46:1; 84:5; 121; Habakkuk 3:19.)

3. How is your strength increased? (*See* Acts 4:31; Romans 8:26; Jude 1:20.)

PRACTICAL APPLICATION

But be ye doers of the word, and not hearers only,
deceiving your own selves.
— James 1:22

1. Matthew 8:28 says that the demonized men living among the tombs were "exceedingly fierce" — they had created an extremely dangerous and treacherous situation. Are you dealing with circumstances like this in your life? How does Jesus' boldness and promise of authority encourage you?

2. The demoniac's situation certainly seemed hopeless. He was mentally, emotionally, and spiritually being tortured. Are you or someone you know in a similar situation? If so, briefly describe the circumstances.

3. According to Romans 15:4 and 13, where does your hope for positive change come from?

TOPIC

Demonic Ferociousness, Self-Destruction, and Fits

SCRIPTURES

1. **Luke 10:19** — Behold, I give unto you power to tread on serpents and scorpions, and over all the power of the enemy....

2. **1 John 4:4** — Ye are of God, little children, and have overcome them: because greater is he that is in you, than he that is in the world.

3. **Mark 5:1-6** — And they came over unto the other side of the sea, into the country of the Gadarenes. And when he was come out of the ship, immediately there met him out of the tombs a man with an unclean spirit. Who had his dwelling among the tombs; and no man could bind him, no, not with chains. Because that he had been often bound with fetters and chains, and the chains had been plucked asunder by him, and the fetters broken in pieces: neither could any man tame him. And always, night and day, he was in the mountains, and in the tombs, crying, and cutting himself with stones. But when he saw Jesus afar off, he ran and worshipped him.

4. **Luke 8:26-29** — And they arrived at the country of the Gadarenes, which is over against Galilee. And when he went forth to land, there met him out of the city a certain man, which had devils long time, and ware no clothes, neither abode in any house, but in the tombs. When he saw Jesus, he cried out, and fell down before him, and with a loud voice said, What have I to do with thee Jesus, thou Son of God most high? I beseech thee, torment me not. (For he had commanded the unclean spirit to come out of the man. For oftentimes it had caught him: and he was kept bound with chains and in fetters; and he brake the bands, and was driven of the devil into the wilderness.)

GREEK WORDS

1. power" — ἐξουσία (*exousia*): authority; denotes one who has received delegated power

2. "tread" — πατέω (*pateo*): to walk on; to trample, to crush; to advance by setting the foot upon

3. "over" — ἐπὶ (*epi*): over; denotes a position of advantage and superiority

4. "power" — δύναμις (*dunamis*): power; dynamic power; superhuman power; depicts the full force of an advancing army

5. "enemy" — ἐχθρός (*echthros*): an irreconcilable hostility; pictures an enemy; someone who is openly hostile; one with a deep-seated hatred; one who is bent on inflicting harm

6. "with an unclean spirit" — ἐν πνεύματι ἀκαθάρτῳ (*en pneumati akatharto*): in the grip of an unclean spirit; in the control of an unclean spirit

7. "met" — ὑπαντάω (*hupantao*): to meet face-to-face; used militarily to denote a hostile meeting

8. "had" — ἔχω (*echo*): to have or to hold; to possess; to suppress
9. "long time" — χρόνῳ ἱκανῷ (*chrono hikano*): chronically; a chronic condition for a prolonged period of time
10. "ware no clothes" — οὐκ ἐνεδύσατο ἱμάτιον (*ouk enedusato himation*): wearing absolutely no clothes; an emphatic statement; no clothes at all; not a shred of clothes
11. "beseech" — δέομαι (*deomai*): to beg, request, beseech, or pray
12. "torment" — βασανίζω (*basanidzo*): to torment or torture; however, the form used in this verse denotes incessant torment and torture
13. "commanded" — παραγγέλλω (*parangello*): to command; the tense means Jesus repeated this command over and over
14. "out" — ἐξέρχομαι (*exerchomai*): to come out; to make an exit
15. "caught" — συναρπάζω (*sunarpadzo*): seize, capture, drag away; depicted some type of physical seizure due to spiritual entities that suddenly seized this man; a medical word to depict seizures
16. "bound" — δέω (*deo*): to bind, tie up, restrict, imprison, or put in chains
17. "was kept" — φυλασσόμενος (*phulassomenos*): continually guarded by protective police or guards
18. "driven" — ἐλαύνω (*elauno*): to drive, as the wind driving ships or clouds; can depict demons driving or coercing those whom they possess; pictures one driven with no rest or respite from torment
19. "wilderness" — ἔρημος (*eremos*): pictures a deserted place; a remote spot; a place that was out of the way; somewhere off the beaten track; an obscure site; isolation; desolation
20. "ran" — τρέχω (*trecho*): to run swiftly; to run speedily, without distraction
21. "worshipped" — προσκυνέω (*proskuneo*): to fall forward to kiss; to fall upon on one's knees in adoration

SYNOPSIS

Just above the eastern shore of the Sea of Galilee there are steep cliffs. In the days of Jesus, these cliffs and the tombs that were nearby were the home of the demoniac of Gadara. This was the place where Jesus stepped out of the boat and was met by this man demonized by a legion of demons.

One would think that he would run *from* Jesus, but that was not the case. The Bible says, "When he saw Jesus afar off, he ran and worshipped him" (Mark 5:6). This verse depicts the demoniac running at full speed and throwing himself down at the feet of Jesus. Why would he run to Jesus? What was he thinking in that moment that would prompt him to hurl himself at Jesus' feet? The answer is found in Luke's gospel, and it's what we will focus on in this lesson.

The emphasis of this lesson:

No matter how ferocious the enemy fights or how many attempts of self-destruction he brings, no one is too far gone or beyond the merciful reach of Jesus' saving power.

Jesus Has Given *You* Authority Over Demons!

Jesus said in Luke 10:19, "Behold, I give unto you power to tread on serpents and scorpions, and over all the power of the enemy; and nothing shall by any means hurt you." In the last few lessons, we have learned from this foundational verse the meaning of several key words.

For instance, the word "behold" in Greek is an exclamation. It was the equivalent of Jesus saying, "Wow! What I'm about to tell you is absolutely amazing. In fact, it's so wonderful, I'm nearly speechless about what I'm about to say. Listen to this: I give you *power....*"

The word "power" here is the Greek word *exousia*, and it means *authority*. Jesus told His disciples, and us, "I am giving you *authority* to tread on serpents and scorpions."

The word "serpents" is the Greek word *ophis*, and it describes *serpents, snakes, or anything related to the devil*. The word "scorpions" can refer to literal *scorpions*, or in this case, it refers to *stinging situations that the enemy brings against us*. Jesus said He has given us power "over" all such circumstances.

The word "over" is the Greek word *epi*, which means *over*. It denotes *a position of advantage and superiority*. Thus Jesus has given you *a superior position of authority* over all the "power" of the enemy. This second mention of the word "power" is the Greek word *dunamis*, and it describes *the full force of an advancing army.*

The Lord used this word to let you know that even if the devil tries to send an army of demons against you, don't be afraid. You have a superior position of advantage over everything Satan tries to bring your way. First John 4:4 declares, "Ye are of God, little children, and have overcome them: because greater is he that is in you, than he that is in the world."

Jesus Met the Demonized Man

Jesus walked in victory over all the power of the enemy, and He demonstrated this clearly when He delivered the demoniac of Gadara. The Bible says, "And they came over unto the other side of the sea, into the country of the Gadarenes. And when he [Jesus] was come out of the ship, immediately there met him out of the tombs a man with an unclean spirit" (Mark 5:1,2).

We have seen that the word "immediately" means *immediately; without delay*. And the word "met" is the Greek word *hupantao*, which is *a military word to denote a hostile meeting*. This demonized man had terrorized the entire region, and according to Matthew's gospel, he was not alone. There were two men. Every time someone tried to pass along the roadway, these men would burst forth from the tombs to threaten and intimidate the people.

When Jesus stepped out of the ship, these demonized men reacted the same way they always had. Scripture says they met Him "out of the tombs." The word "out" is the Greek word *ek*, which is where we get the word *exit*, and the word "tombs" is the Greek word *mnema*, which describes *graves or tombstones*. These men were literally living in the midst of death.

Returning to Mark's account, which focuses on the one man who was most severely possessed, it says he "had his dwelling among the tombs" (Mark 5:3). The word "dwelling" describes *a habitual resident or a habitual habitation*, and the word "among" is the Greek word *en*, which means he was located *right in the middle* of the tombs. That is where he had taken up residency.

The Man Had Been Bound With *Fetters* and *Chains*

Mark 5:3 and 4 goes on to say, "…No man could bind him, no not with chains: because that he had been often bound with fetters and chains, and the chains had been plucked asunder by him, and the fetters broken in pieces...."

The word "chains" is the Greek word *halusis*, which describes *handcuffs*. These restraints were a solid piece of metal that was wrapped around both arms, making it extremely difficult to exert any strength with one's hands. And the word "fetters" is the Greek word *pedes*, and it describes *chains upon the feet*.

The Bible says this man "plucked asunder" the chains around his arms. This phrase "plucked asunder" is the Greek word *diaspao*, and it means *to tear in half; to sever; to tear to pieces*. The phrase "broken in pieces" is the Greek word *suntribo*, which means *to grind or reduce to dust*. Thus, this man was so energized by the demons living in him that he ripped in two the solid metal piece around his arms and beat into dust the metal shackles around his ankles, and he did this multiple times.

He Was Untamable and in Terrible Agony

Not only could the demoniac not be bound, he also could not be *tamed* (*see* Mark 5:4). The word "tame" is the Greek word *damadzo*, which means *to domesticate, to subdue, or to bring under control*. It is a word used to describe *animal trainers who were experts at capturing and domesticating the wildest and most ferocious beasts, such as lions, tigers, and bears*. Although these animals had a tendency to maul or kill a person, skilled trainers were able to take the wildest animals and domesticate them.

By using the word *damadzo* — translated here as "tame" — we see that even the most skilled trainers who were able to subdue and domesticate lions, tigers, and bears could not subdue and domesticate this ferocious man. Thus, he couldn't be bound, he couldn't be tamed, and religious people were powerless to help him. Clearly, he was in a hopeless situation.

Mark 5:5 says, "And always, night and day, he was in the mountains, and in the tombs, crying, and cutting himself with stones." The phrase "always, day and night" means *perpetually*. All day long and all night long, wherever he went, he was "crying" and "cutting" himself. The Greek word for "crying" is *kradzo*, and it describes *an agonizing scream*. The word "cutting" is the Greek word *katakopto*, which means *to gash or to mutilate*.

The demons controlling this man had driven him to attempt suicide repeatedly. Some scholars have speculated that he may have been trying to set himself free. Since no one else had been able to help him, he may have thought that his only way out of his overwhelming situation was through death.

The Man Ran to Jesus and Worshiped Him

Suddenly, in the midst of intense misery, the demonized man saw a glimmer of hope. Mark 5:6 says, "When he saw Jesus afar off, he ran and worshipped him." At first glance, this man's reaction may seem out of character. One would think that, unless he was on a mission to confront with hostility, a person infested with 6,000 demons would run *from* Jesus. But this man ran *toward* Him to worship Him.

The word "ran" is the Greek word *trecho*, which means *to run swiftly; to run speedily, without distraction*. The moment this man saw Jesus a great distance away, he moved his feet as fast as he could to get to Him. Once he was close enough, he threw himself down at Jesus' feet and "worshiped" Him. The word "worshiped" is the Greek word *proskuneo*, and it means *to fall forward to kiss; to fall upon on one's knees in adoration*.

Then without warning, just as the demonized man opened his mouth to ask Jesus for help, the demons seized control of him and began speaking through him. To understand this strange turn of events, we can look to Luke's telling of the story.

Luke's Account Adds a Few Important Details

Luke 8:26 and 27 says that Jesus and His disciples "…arrived at the country of the Gadarenes, which is over against Galilee. And when he [Jesus] went forth to land, there met him out of the city a certain man, which had devils long time, and ware no clothes, neither abode in any house, but in the tombs."

The word "met" in this verse is the Greek word *hupantao* — the same word used in Mark's gospel to describe *a hostile encounter*. Scripture says that this man "had" devils. The word "had" is the Greek word *echo*, which means *to have; to hold; to possess; to suppress*. It carries the idea of being *suppressed and dominated by demons*, and it was for a "long time." The words "long time" in Greek are *chrono hikano*, which means *chronically*. It describes *a chronic condition for a prolonged period of time*. This man's existence had been chronically dominated by demons for a very long time.

In contrast to Mark's gospel, Luke adds that the man "ware no clothes." The Greek meaning of this phrase emphatically states *he was wearing absolutely no clothes — not a shred of clothing*. This is a picture of demonic humiliation. Moreover, the man didn't live in a house; his home was among the tombs. All these details reveal the extreme low level at which he was living.

Luke 8:28 says, "When he saw Jesus, he cried out, and fell down before him...." This verse reveals some of the same details we learned in Mark's account. The phrase "cried out" is the Greek word *kradzo*, which describes *an agonizing scream*. When the man saw Jesus, he yelled in agony and "fell down before him." The words "fell down" are the Greek word *prospipto*, which indicates that the man ran as fast as he could and *threw himself down hard at Jesus' feet*.

The Demons Took Over and Spoke to Jesus

Scripture then says that the man "...with a loud voice said, What have I to do with thee Jesus, thou Son of God most high? I beseech thee, torment me not" (Luke 8:28). It was in that moment that the demons took control of the man's mouth, and instead of the man asking Jesus for help, the demons began to put up a fight and voice their fears.

The word "beseech" in this verse is the Greek word *deomai*, which means *to beg, request, beseech, or pray*. Basically, the unclean spirit in this man was praying and begging Jesus not to "torment" him. The word "torment" is the Greek word *basanidzo*, which means *to torment or torture*. What's significant is that the form used in this verse denotes *incessant torment and torture*.

What was Jesus doing over and over that was tormenting this unclean spirit? The answer is found in Luke 8:29. It says, "(For he had commanded the unclean spirit to come out of the man. For oftentimes it had caught him: and he was kept bound with chains and in fetters; and he brake the bands, and was driven of the devil into the wilderness.)"

Notice the word "commanded" in this verse. It is the Greek word *parangello*, which means *to command*. The tense means *Jesus repeated this command over and over and over again*. This lets us know that the first time Jesus spoke to the unclean spirit and told it to come out of the man, it didn't come out. Usually, when Jesus spoke to demons, they obeyed immediately. He would cast them out with just a word. In this case, however, the evil spirit wouldn't budge. Therefore, Jesus began to interrogate it by saying, "What is your name?"

The unclean spirit answered, "…My name is Legion: for we are many" (Mark 5:9). Hence, the reason the unclean spirit refused to leave was that it wasn't alone. This one man was filled with an infestation of 6,000 demons. To break their stubbornness, Jesus kept commanding the demons again and again and again to come out of the man, and He didn't leave the man until those demons fully obeyed Him.

The Man Was Oftentimes 'Caught' by the Demons

Looking again at Luke 8:29, it says that the demons oftentimes "caught him." This word "caught" is quite significant. It is the Greek word *sunarpadzo*, and it means *to seize, capture, or drag away*. It depicted *some type of physical seizure due to spiritual entities that suddenly seized this man*. The word *sunarpadzo* is actually a medical word used to depict *seizures*.

To be clear, not everyone who has epilepsy has demons. However, those who are demonized like this man from Gadara often exhibit seizure-like episodes. This demonized man had moments in his life when he was in control of himself and his thinking. Such was the case the day Jesus arrived in the vicinity of the Gadarenes. When he saw Christ, he ran to Him and threw himself down to worship Him. He knew that if he didn't move fast and reach out to Jesus for help, the demons would seize him and stop him from getting to Jesus.

But the moment the man opened his mouth to ask Jesus for help, the demons "caught" him and threw him into a demonic seizure. Instead of him speaking, the demons took control of his voice and began speaking through him.

He Was 'Driven' Into the 'Wilderness'

Luke 8:29 goes on to say that after the man broke free from the chains and fetters, he was "driven of the devil into the wilderness." The word driven is the Greek word *elauno*, and it means *to drive, as the wind driving ships or clouds*. It can depict *demons driving or coercing those whom they possess*, and it pictures *one driven with no rest or respite from torment*.

Also notice the word "wilderness." It is the Greek word *eremos*, and it pictures *a deserted place; a remote spot; a place that is out of the way;*

somewhere off the beaten track; an obscure, isolated, desolate site. The idea of being "driven" into the "wilderness" is a vivid picture of what the devil desires to do to people. He wants to drive them relentlessly, without rest, out into places of deep isolation. He wants to wear them out mentally, emotionally, physically, and spiritually and keep them away from anyone who could help them.

Thankfully, Jesus saw right into this worn out, miserable man's heart. Even though the man couldn't verbalize what he wanted to say, Jesus could see his faith and his desire to be set free, and He responded accordingly. Jesus said, "…The one who comes to Me I will most certainly not cast out [I will never, no never, reject one of them who comes to Me]" (John 6:37 *AMPC*).

STUDY QUESTIONS

Study to shew thyself approved unto God, a workman that needeth not to be ashamed, rightly dividing the word of truth.
— 2 Timothy 2:15

Along with exercising our God-given authority over all the power of the enemy, we also must learn to recognize and resist the devil's attempts to gain entrance into our lives. God instructs us clearly on this in His Word.

1. According to Ephesians 4:26 and 27, what is one of the major ways Satan gains access into our lives? What practical steps can you take to shut the door on him in this area of your life?

2. In First Peter 5:8 and 9, the Lord warns us of the devil's eagerness to take us down. What are you to do to stand against the line of attack mentioned in this passage? (Also *consider* James 4:7,8.)

PRACTICAL APPLICATION

But be ye doers of the word, and not hearers only, deceiving your own selves.
—James 1:22

1. One of the tactics of the enemy is to *drive* us just as he had driven the demoniac of Gadara. Take a moment to stop and think: *Am I being driven by the enemy in some area of my life? Am I being pushed and*

pressed to perform without any rest to the point I feel tormented? If the answer is yes, where in your life is it happening?

2. Take time now to pray and say, "Lord, thank You for exposing the enemy's activity. Please forgive me for giving him any place to operate in my life (*see* Ephesians 4:26,27). Show me what I need to do differently to experience regular times of rest in You. In Jesus' name, amen." Be still and listen. What is the Lord speaking to you?

LESSON 5

TOPIC
Demonic Submission to Jesus

SCRIPTURES

1. **Luke 10:19** — Behold, I give unto you power to tread on serpents and scorpions, and over all the power of the enemy....

2. **Mark 5:1-15, 18-20** — And they came over unto the other side of the sea, into the country of the Gadarenes. And when he was come out of the ship, immediately there met him out of the tombs a man with an unclean spirit. Who had his dwelling among the tombs; and no man could bind him, no, not with chains. Because that he had been often bound with fetters and chains, and the chains had been plucked asunder by him, and the fetters broken in pieces: neither could any man tame him. And always, night and day, he was in the mountains, and in the tombs, crying, and cutting himself with stones. But when he saw Jesus afar off, he ran and worshipped him. And cried with a loud voice, and said, What have I to do with thee, Jesus, thou Son of the most high God? I adjure thee by God, that thou torment me not. For he said into him, Come out of the man, thou unclean spirit. And he asked him, What is thy name? And he answered, saying, My name is Legion: for we are many. And he besought him much that he would not send them away out of the country. Now there was there nigh unto the mountains a great herd of swine feeding. And all the devils besought him, saying, Send us into the swine, that we may enter into them. And forthwith Jesus gave them leave. And the unclean spirits went out, and entered into the swine: and the herd ran violently

down a steep place into the sea, (they were about two thousand;) and were choked in the sea. And they that fed the swine fled, and told it in the city, and in the country. And they went out to see what it was that was done. And they come to Jesus, and see him that was possessed with the devil, and had the legion, sitting, and clothed, and in his right mind: and they were afraid. And when he was come into the ship, he that had been possessed with the devil prayed him that he might be with him. Howbeit Jesus suffered him not, but saith unto him, Go home to thy friends, and tell them how great things the Lord hath done for thee, and hath had compassion on thee. And he departed, and began to publish in Decapolis how great things Jesus had done for him: and all men did marvel.

GREEK WORDS

1. "power" — ἐξουσία (*exousia*): authority; denotes one who has received delegated power

2. "tread" — πατέω (*pateo*): to walk on; to trample, to crush; to advance by setting the foot upon

3. "over" — ἐπὶ (*epi*): over; denotes a position of advantage and superiority

4. "power" — δύναμις (*dunamis*): power; dynamic power; superhuman power; depicts the full force of an advancing army

5. "enemy" — ἐχθρός (*echthros*): an irreconcilable hostility; pictures an enemy; someone who is openly hostile; one with a deep-seated hatred; one who is bent on inflicting harm

6. "with an unclean spirit" — ἐν πνεύματι ἀκαθάρτῳ (*en pneumati akatharto*): in the grip of an unclean spirit; in the control of an unclean spirit

7. "ran" — τρέχω (*trecho*): to run swiftly; to run speedily, without distraction

8. "worshipped" — προσκυνέω (*proskuneo*): to fall forward to kiss; to fall upon on one's knees in adoration

9. "adjure" — ὁρκίζω (*horkidzo*): to solemnly plead; used in a religious sense to plead to God

10. "torment" — βασανίζω (*basanidzo*): to torment or torture; however, the form used in this verse denotes incessant torment and torture

11. "said"— ἔλεγεν (*elegen*): the Greek tense means, "He kept on saying…"

12. "out"— ἐκ (*ek*): out; root word from which we get the word "exit"

13. "asked"— ἐπερωτάω (*eperotao*): to interrogate; tense depicts an ongoing interrogation

14. "legion"— Λεγιὼν (*Legion*): a military term that denoted at least 6,000 Roman soldiers

15. "he besought"— παρακαλέω (*parakaleo*): to passionately call out; to plead; to beckon; to beg; denotes a word of prayer

16. "swine"— χοῖρος (*choiros*): in this verse, the plural form for a pig or hog, which was considered to be the lowest, basest, and most unclean of animals

17. "went out"— ἐξέρχομαι (*exerchomai*): to come out; to make an exit

18. "entered into"— εἰσέρχομαι (*eiserchomai*): to enter into; to travel into; to go into

19. "ran violently down"— ὁρμάω (*hormao*): to uncontrollably and wildly rush forward

20. "choked"— πνίγω (*pnigo*): to choke; to strangle; to wring one's neck; to take one by the throat

21. "sitting"— καθήμενον (*kathemenon*): to be seated in a restful position; the tense means continuously seated

22. "clothed"— ἱματισμένον (*himatismenon*): to be dressed, as any normal person; the tense means continuously dressed

23. "right mind"— σωφρονοῦντα (*sophronounta*): to be of sound mind; to be reasonable; to be balanced and levelheaded in the way one thinks; to think rationally; the tense means a continuous action of being in his right mind.

24. "house"— οἶκος (*oikos*): a home; a residence

25. "friends"— πρὸς τοὺς σούς (*pros tous sous*): to your own; to your own people

26. "publish"— κηρύσσω (*kerusso*): to preach, proclaim, declare, announce, or herald a message; pictures a message proclaimed by the official spokesman or herald of a king whose job was to speak on behalf of the king

27. "done"— ποιέω (*poieo*): to do; to make; to create; the tense depicts something made complete

28. "marvel" — θαυμάζω (*thaumadzo*): to wonder; to be at a loss for words; to be shocked and amazed; to be bewildered

SYNOPSIS

By far, one of the most dramatic demonstrations of Jesus' power and authority took place in the Gadarenes, which is located on the eastern side of the Sea of Galilee. Shortly after stilling a violent storm on the sea, Jesus stepped out of the boat and onto the shore and was immediately met by two demonized men (*see* Matthew 8:28). One of these men was much worse off than the other, being in the grip of nearly 6,000 demons. Although the demons stubbornly resisted, Jesus did not leave until they obeyed His command and vacated the man. Today, the remains of a monastery built in the Fifth Century still stand on this sacred site, commemorating the mighty deliverance that took place.

The emphasis of this lesson:

Jesus is fully devoted to seeing people set free from the grip of demonic activity. Regardless of the size or strength of the enemy's army, the devil and demons must submit to the authority of Christ.

You Have Been Vested With Christ-Given Authority

In Luke 10:19, Jesus said, "Behold, I give unto you power to tread on serpents and scorpions, and over all the power of the enemy: and nothing shall by any means hurt you." When Jesus said, "Behold," the Greek here actually means, "Wow! Listen to what I'm about to tell you. It is so amazing. I give you *power*...."

The word "power" is the Greek word *exousia*, which means *authority*. Thus, Jesus said, "I give you authority." This lets us know that when we stand against the devil, we don't operate in our own authority. We operate in Christ-given authority, and it is so powerful that we can stand victoriously against serpents, scorpions, and over all the power of the enemy.

The word "over" in this verse is the Greek word *epi*, which means *upon*. In this case, however, it describes *a superior position of advantage*. We have a position of advantage because we have Christ-given authority. We are the ones who are superior in spiritual conflicts because Christ has given us His authority over all the "power" of the enemy.

The second appearance of the word "power" is the Greek word *dunamis*, which describes the *full might of an advancing army*. This means that even if the devil marshals all of his best troops against you at one time, you still have a position of advantage because of your Christ-given authority.

That's His promise to each and every one of us. With that in mind, let's review the story of the demoniac in Mark 5.

An Unclean Spirit Had a Death-Grip on This Man

Mark 5:1 and 2 says, "…They came over unto the other side of the sea, into the country of the Gadarenes. And when he [Jesus] was come out of the ship, immediately there met him out of the tombs a man with an unclean spirit."

"Unclean" is the Greek word *akatharto*, and it describes *something vile, foul, or filthy*.

"With and unclean spirit" in Greek actually means *in the grip of an unclean spirit* or *in the control of an unclean spirit*. This man didn't have the unclean spirit; the unclean spirit had him.

Mark 5:3-5 says, "Who had his dwelling among the tombs; and no man could bind him, no, not with chains. Because that he had been often bound with fetters and chains, and the chains had been plucked asunder by him, and the fetters broken in pieces: neither could any man tame him. And always, night and day, he was in the mountains, and in the tombs, crying, and cutting himself with stones."

"Always, night and day" in Greek means *perpetually, in the nighttime and in the daytime*. Wherever this man was — in the mountains or in the tombs — he was in misery day and night.

"Crying" is the Greek word *kradzo*, which describes *an agonizing scream*.

"Cutting" is the Greek word *katakopto*, and it means *to cut downward; to gash downward; to mutilate*. The demons inside this man had driven him to the point of self-destruction. Some scholars believe he was trying to take his life to set himself free from his deplorable situation.

We know from Luke's gospel that this man was naked, roaming the countryside without a stitch of clothing. The enemy had stolen this man's dignity and driven him to a place of humiliation. He was no longer living with his family in his home. He was living in the wilderness — isolated in torment.

The Demoniac Made a Mad Dash Toward Jesus

We saw in our last lesson that the demons living in this man oftentimes "caught" him (*see* Luke 8:28), which is *a medical term describing seizure-like episodes.* This tells us how the demons manifested. Just as a person with epilepsy has times when he or she seems normal and then suddenly experiences unannounced seizures, there were times when this man was in control of himself, but then was suddenly thrown into a demonic fit.

When Jesus first showed up in the country of the Gadarenes, this man was in control of his thinking. He recognized Jesus and ran to Him immediately with the hope of being set free. He knew if he didn't move quickly, the demons would seize him and throw him into a fit. Thus, he literally was trying to outrun another demonic manifestation.

Mark 5:6 says, "But when he saw Jesus afar off, he ran and worshipped him." The word "ran" is the Greek word *trecho*, which means *to run swiftly; to run speedily, without distraction.* The word "worshiped" is the Greek word *proskuneo*, and it means *to fall forward to kiss; to fall upon on one's knees in adoration.* When this tormented man saw Jesus, he moved his feet as fast as he could and threw himself down at Jesus' feet in worship.

The Day the Devil Prayed

However, when the man opened his mouth to ask Jesus for help, the unclean spirit seized him and began speaking through him. Mark 5:7 says it "...cried with a loud voice, and said, What have I to do with thee, Jesus, thou Son of the most high God? I adjure thee by God, that thou torment me not."

Notice the word "adjure." It is the Greek word *horkidzo*, and it means *to solemnly plead.* This word was used in a religious sense to plead to God. The unclean spirit living in this man was literally praying to Jesus, begging Him to cease and desist His "torment."

The Greek word for "torment" here is *basanidzo*, which means *to torment or torture*. However, the form used in this verse denotes *incessant torment and torture*. Jesus was doing something again and again that was causing this unclean spirit to feel tremendous pressure. Verse 8 reveals Jesus' actions: "For he said unto him, Come out of the man, thou unclean spirit."

The word "said" here is the Greek word *elegen*, and the tense means that at first, "he kept on saying." The reason Jesus kept on saying and saying and saying, "Come out of the man" was, the evil spirit wouldn't budge. When others had tried to help this man and were unable to, they gave up and walked away. But Jesus didn't. He stayed with this man until the unclean spirit came "out."

The Greek word *ek*, translated here as "out," is the root word from which we get the word "exit." Jesus was literally commanding this evil spirit *to make an exit* from the man. Interestingly, the word "from" is the Greek word *apo*, which carries the idea of *distance*. Essentially, Jesus was ordering this foul, filthy spirit to *make an exit from this man and to put distance between the two of them*.

Jesus Interrogated the Evil Spirit

Normally, when Jesus came across a person bound by an unclean spirit, He spoke the word, and the demon fled. There was no conversation. In fact, He usually commanded demons to be silent. In this situation, however, the evil spirit wouldn't budge. Therefore, "He [Jesus] asked him What is thy name? And he answered, saying, My name is Legion: for we are many" (Mark 5:9).

Notice the word "asked." It is the Greek word *eperotao*, which means *to interrogate*. The tense depicts an ongoing interrogation. After Jesus put pressure on the unclean spirit, it revealed that its name was "Legion," which is *a military term that denoted at least 6,000 Roman soldiers*. The demon talking to Jesus at that moment indicated that there were 6,000 demons inside this man. It said, "for we are many," which means, *"We are a vast multitude."*

Mark 5:10 says, "He [the unclean spirit] besought him much that he would not send them away out of the country." Notice, this was still just *one* demon speaking to Jesus. The phrase "he besought" is the Greek word *parakaleo*, which means *to passionately call out; to plead; to beckon; to beg*. It denotes *a word of prayer*. Here again, we see the enemy praying and pleading with Jesus as it felt the incessant pressure of the Lord's command.

The Demons Requested Asylum in the Swine

The Bible says, "Now there was there nigh unto the mountains a great herd of swine feeding. And all the devils besought him, saying, Send us into the swine, that we may enter into them" (Mark 5:11,12). Where did the demons ask to go? Into a herd of "swine," which in this verse is the plural form for *a pig or hog*. Swine were considered to be *the lowest, basest, and most unclean of animals.*

At that point, "all the devils besought" Jesus. In other words, the situation shifted from one demon doing the talking in verse 10 to *all the demons* praying and pleading with Jesus in verse 12. Imagine the sound of 6,000 devils all speaking simultaneously, begging to be sent into a herd of pigs.

Demons desire to live in something, and if they can't inhabit a person, they will live in an animal, such as a dog or a pig. "And forthwith Jesus gave them leave. And the unclean spirits went out, and entered into the swine: and the herd ran violently down a steep place into the sea, (they were about two thousand;) and were choked in the sea" (Mark 5:13).

Thus, the unclean spirits "went out" — the Greek word *exerchomai*, which means *to come out or to make an exit* — and they "entered into" the swine. The phrase "entered into" is the Greek word *eiserchomai*, which means *to enter into; to travel into; to go into.* If there were 2,000 pigs and 6,000 demons, it means each pig likely became a home to three demons.

How Did the Swine Respond?

Scripture says the pigs "ran violently down a steep place into the sea." The phrase "ran violently down" is the Greek word *hormao*, and it means *to uncontrollably and wildly rush forward.* Under the control of 6,000 demons, the swine were driven into the sea where they were "choked." The Greek word for "choked" is *pnigo*, which means *to choke; to strangle; to wring one's neck; to take one by the throat.*

It is important to see that when these 6,000 demons were living in *one man*, the man was still alive. Even though they had tried multiple times to get him to take his life, they were unsuccessful. This tells us that even if a person is infested with demons, he or she still has a free will to choose to seek help. God can see the desire of a person's heart — even if they cannot verbalize their request.

Animals, such as the herd of 2,000 swine, don't have a will. The moment the demons went into the pigs, they went crazy and were immediately driven to destruction. That is the purpose and mode of operation for evil spirits — they destroy whatever they can destroy.

What Was the People's Response?

Mark 5:14 and 15 go on to say, "And they that fed the swine fled, and told it in the city, and in the country. And they went out to see what it was that was done. And they come to Jesus, and see him that was possessed with the devil, and had the legion, sitting, and clothed, and in his right mind: and they were afraid."

The Scripture tells us that the townspeople came out to "see" for themselves what had happened to the man who had been filled with demons. The word "see" is the Greek word *theoreo*, which means *to gaze at or to look at* — it is where we get the word "theater." The use of this word indicates that the people came out to view in amazement what had actually taken place in this man's life.

The phrase "that was possessed of the devil" in Greek actually means, *the one who had been habitually demonized; the one who had had the legion*. The 6,000 demons were now gone, and the man was "sitting, and clothed, and in his right mind…" (Mark 5:15).

The word "sitting" in Greek is *kathemenon*, and it means *to be seated in a restful position*. The tense indicates *continuously seated*. The word "clothed" in Greek indicates *to be dressed, as any normal person*. The tense means *continuously dressed*.

Instead of being driven by the devil, this man was now sitting at peace. Instead of being naked, he was fully dressed and "in his right mind," which means *to be of sound mind; to be reasonable; to be balanced and levelheaded in the way one thinks; to think rationally*. Again, just as with the words "sitting" and "clothed," the tense here means *a continuous action of being in his right mind*. When the people saw the drastic change in this man, they were afraid and urged Jesus to leave.

The Delivered Man Became a Preacher in His Land

Mark 5:18 says, "And when he [Jesus] was come into the ship, he that had been possessed with the devil prayed him that he might be with him." The man who had been delivered of the legion of demons was so grateful to Jesus for what He did that he begged to be allowed to stay with Him.

In verse 19 it says, "Howbeit Jesus suffered him not, but saith unto him, Go home to thy friends, and tell them how great things the Lord hath done for thee, and hath had compassion on thee." The word "home" here is the Greek word *oikos*, and it describes *a home* or *a residence*. And the word "friends" specifically refers to *one's own people*. Jesus told the man to return to the physical home he had once lived in prior to the demonic infestation, and to reunite with those who were his own.

Accordingly, the Bible says, "And he departed, and began to publish in Decapolis how great things Jesus had done for him: and all men did marvel" (Mark 5:20). The word "publish" is the Greek word *kerusso*, which means *to preach, proclaim, declare, announce, or herald a message*. Essentially, this formerly demonized man became *a preacher*, telling people everywhere he went about the miraculous delivering power of Jesus Christ.

And "all men did marvel." The word "marvel" is the Greek word *thaumadzo*, which means *to wonder; to be at a loss for words; to be shocked and amazed; to be bewildered*. The people in Decapolis knew of the legendary demoniac and how he had terrorized the region. When they heard his testimony and saw firsthand what Jesus had done, they were speechless. No one had ever seen anything like it.

Jesus is still setting people free today! If you or someone you know is bound in any way, don't give up. Press into Jesus' presence. He is ready, willing, and more than able to bring true deliverance to anyone who is held captive.

STUDY QUESTIONS

Study to shew thyself approved unto God, a workman that needeth not to be ashamed, rightly dividing the word of truth.
— 2 Timothy 2:15

1. When Jesus encountered the demoniac controlled by 6,000 demons, they resisted His command to make an exit. How did Jesus confront

their stubbornness — what did He continue to do again and again until they obeyed?

2. What does this fact say to you personally about your fight against the enemy? (*Consider* Galatians 6:9.)

3. Even though the demonized man was unable to ask Jesus for deliverance, Jesus was able to see into his heart and know his desires. Carefully read Matthew 6:8; Jeremiah 17:9,10; and Romans 8:26 and 27, which resonate this theme. Write down what the Holy Spirit speaks to you.

4. Mark 5:14-17 describe the townspeople's reaction to the demoniac's miraculous deliverance (also *consider* Matthew 8:33,34; Luke 8:37). What does this tell you about people's responses to the supernatural work of Jesus even today?

PRACTICAL APPLICATION

But be ye doers of the word, and not hearers only,
deceiving your own selves.
—James 1:22

The demoniac of Gadara was in the grip of 6,000 demons. Skilled animal trainers couldn't tame him; neither could he be bound by chains. In society's eyes, he was most likely seen as a lost cause — even by the religious people of the day.

1. Do you know someone who falls into this category — he or she seems to be too far gone to be helped?

2. Since this man with 6,000 demons living inside him could be delivered, what does that say to you about the person you feel is too far gone? How does it ignite hope and stir up faith?

3. Take some time to reflect on what you learned in this series and pray boldly in faith for the one who desperately needs to be set free from the enemy's control.

A Prayer To Receive Salvation

If you've never received Jesus as your Savior and Lord, now is the time for you to experience the new life Jesus wants to give you! To receive God's gift of salvation that can be obtained through Jesus alone, pray this prayer from your heart:

Jesus, I repent of my sin and receive You as my Savior and Lord. Wash away my sin with Your precious blood and make me completely new. I thank You that my sin is removed, and Satan no longer has any right to lay claim on me. Through Your empowering grace, I faithfully promise that I will serve You as my Lord for the rest of my life.

If you just prayed this prayer of salvation, you are born again! You are a brand-new creation in Christ! Would you please let us know of your decision by going to **renner.org/salvation**? We would love to connect with you and pray for you as you begin your new life in Christ.

Scriptures for further study: John 3:16; John 14:6; Acts 4:12; Ephesians 1:7; Hebrews 10:19,20; 1 Peter 1:18,19; Romans 10:9,10; Colossians 1:13; 2 Corinthians 5:17; Romans 6:4; 1 Peter 1:3

Notes

_____

_____

_____

_____

_____

_____

_____

_____

_____

_____

_____

_____

_____

_____

_____

_____

_____

_____

_____

_____

_____

_____

_____

_____

_____

_____

_____

_____

CLAIM YOUR FREE RESOURCE!

As a way of introducing you further to the teaching ministry of Rick Renner, we would like to send you FREE of charge his teaching, "How To Receive a Miraculous Touch From God" on CD or as an MP3 download.

In His earthly ministry, Jesus commonly healed *all* who were sick of *all* their diseases. In this profound message, learn about the manifold dimensions of Christ's wisdom, goodness, power, and love toward all humanity who came to Him in faith with their needs.

☑ **YES, I want to receive Rick Renner's monthly teaching letter!**

Simply scan the QR code to claim this resource or go to:
renner.org/claim-your-free-offer

Connect

WITH US!